SARSAPARILLA *and* ME

SARSAPARILLA *and* ME

Lenora 'Lennie' Pfister Parkins

Xulon Press

Xulon Press
2301 Lucien Way #415
Maitland, FL 32751
407.339.4217
www.xulonpress.com

Paperback ISBN-13: 978-1-66282-731-0
Hard Cover ISBN-13: 978-1-66282-732-7
Ebook ISBN-13: 978-1-66282-734-1

TABLE OF CONTENTS

INTRODUCTION

What a joy for me to bring you along on a journey of a lifetime, of memories and stories of my life. My journey begins in a small town in Montana, continues with some college fun, and includes some unique jobs like working for Siegfried and Roy in Las Vegas. I wanted to share these stories because I believe life gives us gems of ups and downs and pie-eating contests. My desire is to leave a collection of memoires that I hold dear to my heart, because they are filled with friends I love, family I adore, and experiences that are unique to me but worthy to share. So, grab a Sarsaparilla to sip on and enjoy my collection of short stories.

Part 1

A LIFETIME

Chapter 1

PFISTER'S GROCERY STORE

I was raised by my parents, Emil and Mabel Pfister. We lived in a small neighborhood grocery store, kind of what you would call a "Mom and Pop" store. We carried lots of different things, like canned goods, fresh produce, bottled soda pop, dairy products, bakery items, and freshly sliced lunchmeat. One of my jobs was to hand-pack ice cream into pint and quart containers, and I made milkshakes upon request. We also had a comic book area on shelves, which my sister and I loved to read when we could take a break.

Our living quarters joined the store, so when we were in our dining room behind the store and the bell rang, which we had over the door, we could hear when someone came in. One of us would jump up right away and go out to wait on them. Since the store was in a small area called Lower Sun River, people did not have to go very far to get groceries. We did a lot of business.

The Lower Sun River area was close to the Missouri River. One time the Missouri River flooded, and it came up several feet into the store. To my amazement, the National Guard had boats going around to help people get away from the water. They stopped at our store and put my sister, Shirley, and me in the boat. My mom and dad would not go because they wanted to stay at the store so thieves would not come in and make a big mess and take things. We went on a boat to my aunt's house across town. Our parents joined us a day later when the water finally rose too deep for them to stay. We stayed there for a couple of weeks till the water went down, and my mom and dad could clean up the store.

There was a lot of mud left after the water subsided, which was an incredible amount of work to clean up. But it was a family store, and we had customers to take care of, so we worked hard to get back up and running. In a small way, we felt like we had an essential purpose in our community. Unfortunately, this was not the last time the river rose to destruction. Fifteen years after this flood, another one came with a vengeance and covered the store over the roof. Thankfully, this was well past our family owning it, but that Missouri River is a force for sure.

In the summer, we had Mexican people working in the beet fields for some farmers, and they would come with a truckload of people to buy groceries. My mother would walk around the store to show them things they could not find. They all spoke Spanish, so it was hard to help them. Since they came every summer, my mom decided to take classes and learn how to speak Spanish for the future. When the next summer came, she did a super job of communicating with them; and they were so happy to have someone that could help them pick out the groceries.

One of my favorite parts about the store was our soda fountain. We had pop machines to get different types of drinks in glasses or paper cups to take out. We had various soda pops, including Root Beer, Coke©, 7-UP©, Pepsi©, but the most unusual soda was a green-colored fizzy drink called Sarsaparilla! It was the number one drink that we sold. Maybe because it was impressive, eh? I always loved that name, and it was the inspiration for the title of my book. It brings me many memories, and I wanted to acquaint you with this unique drink.

Running a family grocery store was not all we did. One fun thing we used to do was have slumber parties. My sister and I had permission to every once in a while, invite friends over. Shirley was about ten years old then, and I was two years older. After we closed up the store about ten at night, and my parents went to bed, we made beds on the living room floor. We had a great time going out into the grocery store for treats. My parents said we could have whatever we wanted, so some of the kids got popsicles, fudgesicles, bottles of pop, lunch meat to eat right out of their hands, watermelons, fresh cherries, or fruit. Sometimes they even wanted canned goods like shrimp, olives, or such. We would open the cans with a can opener and eat right out of the can. They thought that was lots of fun!

We could also go to the comic book rack and pick out funny books of Superman and all kinds of other ones, and lay in our beds and read them. We stayed up quite late, but everyone had a perfect time!

My Family: dad Emil, mom Mabel,
oldest sister Betty, sister Shirley and me.

My dad was born in Switzerland. He was a happy man and did lots of fun things; like when a neighbor had a baby or birthday, he would take a box of goodies over to them. Because of that, everyone called him "The Mayor of Lower Sun River." The highlight of what he did was to dress in costume to be Santa Claus. Even then, the two of us girls didn't know about it. My mother helped him get dressed up on Christmas Eve, and he snuck out of the house and went around the neighborhood and passed out candy and gifts. When he came home, he snuck in the back door so we would not see him and ruin the idea that there was a Santa Claus. Then, later, we got to open our Christmas presents and have fudge, cookies, and candy canes.

My mom, baby sister Shirley and me.

I also had an older sister, Betty, who was ten years older than me. One time, she had some Native American friends from school, and they had horses and were good riders. Once in a while, they would come over with their horses bareback, meaning no saddles, and wanted Betty to ride with them. She was sixteen years old and a pretty blonde girl; and the boys liked her. They would bring an extra horse for her, and she would get a running start from the back of the horse and leap right up onto the horse. And they would run like a bat out of hell!

Chapter 2

MSU – THOSE
WERE THE DAYS

In the summer going into the fall of 1958, I was scurrying around to make sure I was all ready for college. I had to get my haircut a couple of weeks before I left and packed my two suitcases. (Wow, did I think that was all I needed?) The time had come, and we were on the road to a new unknown. I was headed to Bozeman to Montana State University.

I rode with a friend, and the drive was only about three hours long. When we got there, the university had already assigned dorms and rooms to us. I checked in and went to my room. Then it hit me. I couldn't believe I was away from home for what was going to be a long time. All of a sudden, the little town grocery store seemed so far away.

The next day there was a knock on my door. I opened it, and, to my surprise, it was my new roommate! It was funny because she lived right there in the university town, Bozeman, but she wanted to leave her house and make-believe she was someplace out of the state. Her name was Niki.

I had heard of sororities and was kind of interested in seeing more about them. Niki told me that a person had to be referred by a former sorority sister or other people. I wanted to check it out and, since we had to apply, I sat down at my typewriter and wrote the details of my life—things like my name, what schools I had attended at home, and other essential information. I left the typed page on my desk, and Niki and I left to go to classes that following day.

To my surprise, Niki's mother stopped over and brought us clean laundry and some cookies. Without me knowing it, she bent over and read the material I had written on the typewriter. A few days later, I got a letter in the Alpha Omicron Pi Sorority mail to invite me there the following evening. Little did I know that Niki's mother copied down all the things I had written about my life. Because of that, her mother vouched for me as a candidate to be a member of the sorority. I was thrilled because they can only take a certain amount of gals. We had twenty-five of us in the pledge group.

We had to live in the dorm for the first year; then we got to live in the sorority house for the remainder of our college days, which amounted to three more years. It was quite an experience.

As the years went by at MSU, I majored in home economics and minored in science. I won a couple of awards for good grades, got rides home every few months, and then had the summers off. In my senior year, I was voted secretary of the class, so I had a little extra work to do, but it was very satisfying. But my time at school was not all academic. There were plenty of shenanigans to be had by all.

In my senior year, I knew a fraternity boy, John, an engineering major. He tutored me in challenging subjects, such as chemistry and math, and we became terrific friends. His fraternity house was the back of our AOPi house; our sorority and fraternity houses played plenty of pranks on each other.

One time, John invited me on a date with several other couples. We were going on a trip to Yellowstone Park, which is only about forty miles from our school campus. The guys were from the fraternity, and I was John's date. We all took in the scenery, animals, and hot pools. It was breathtaking as always. Our goal this evening was to see the enormous geyser, Old Faithful, in the middle of Yellowstone Park. We arrived and walked up to the area to watch the geyser. There were benches circled all around the spout to allow people front-row seats to the fantastic, natural show. There were many park rangers to assist people in getting seated.

Let me remind you we were young college students out for a night out. Imagine many people from all over the world sitting on these benches to watch Old Faithful. When the geyser started to flow, one of the fraternity boys had brought a BIG tractor wheel. He went a few feet closer and pushed the wheel down in the dirt. Then he put his hands on the wheel as the geyser started to go up. His hands began to go around the wheel as if he controlled the geyser, as if he was opening a valve. As the geyser went up farther and faster, he started going fast on the wheel. It looked so real, and the people couldn't stop laughing. As you can imagine, we laughed about this for a long time!

Monday, Nov. 21, 1960   Great Falls Tribune 19

Local Students Named In College Who's Who

Lenora Pfister and George T. Molen, both of Great Falls, have been chosen members of Who's

GEORGE T. MOLEN

LENORA PFISTER

member of Alpha Phi Gamma journalism honorary and was editor of the MSC Handbook. She

Who Among Students in American Universities and Colleges from Montana State College.

Members are selected their senior year on the basis of scholarship, activities, citizenship, service to MSC and promise of future usefulness.

A home economics major, Miss Pfister is the daughter of Mrs. Mable Pfister, 1426 Central Ave. W., and is MSC Student Senate publicity chairman.

She is the recipient of a home demonstration s c h o l a r s h i p, a

is affiliated with Alpha Omicron Pi sorority.

Molen, the son of Mr. and Mrs. Reid L. Molen, 3108 3rd Ave. S., is a commerce major and was a star of the Bobcat football team the past two seasons. Playing left halfback, Molen was the Bobcats' leading ground gainer last season, and was one of the team's top ground gainers this season until sidelined with a broken hand last month. He is affiliated with Sigma Alpha Epsilon fraternity.

Chapter 3

AOPI HOUSE

AOPi House Entrance in 1959.

The AOPi house had a balcony in the back of it. It had a railing around it, but no way to go inside except the door we came in and out. Back to back were the two fraternity houses: our AOPi house and the Kappa Sig house. There was a parking lot between the two places for the students that had cars.

The gals loved to bring out a towel and have on their bathing suits and sunbathe out there in the sun. One afternoon, when we all were coming home from classes, we heard a funny noise. We looked up at the balcony from the sidewalk going to the house. Oh my gosh, when we got closer, guess what it was? Someone had put two GOATS up there.

The poor goats didn't know what to do, so they just kept running from one end to the other, making funny noises. We suspected our friendly frat neighbors. The house mother called the police and had them taken care of it. Of course, it was funny for years!

Another time, our sorority sisters came in second for the women's baseball tournament. One Saturday, we were invited to the finals to play with the other team. My mother had let me bring a car to college my senior year, and I parked it to the side of the front of the AOPi House. About five of us had to get going and meet the other team for the game. We all had casual slacks on, and the weather was warm. We all piled into the car, and I started it up.

BUT... the car wouldn't move, what happened? One of the girls got out and checked it. She found out the problem! The frat boys had put all four of my tires up on cement blocks! They were all looking out the third-floor window from their house, just laughing aloud. So, to make a long story short, we didn't have time to get to the game so we didn't go.

AOPi Sorority Sisters 1960.

Chapter 4

ZORRO

Remember the show called *Zorro*? The character of Zorro was a mysterious, masked man dressed in black that would disappear into the night. He could sneak around, undetected, and get revenge by way of the sword against the men who killed his brother.

Well, I had just seen the movie about Zorro, so he was on my mind. I do not know what possessed me to want to play a little trick on the girls in the sorority house, but in my mind, this seemed like a fabulous idea. I mean, it wasn't going to harm anyone; I just wanted to have a little prankster fun.

At the time, forty girls and one house mother were living there at the house. There was an open slot where the mail came through and landed on the floor right inside the front door.

I looked around late one evening to see if everyone was settled in their rooms at bedtime. It was tranquil. I wrote a note and set it on the floor right where the mail came in. I had written a letter that said "WATCH OUT ...I AM COMING FOR YOU" - ZORRO!

I started to make different notes off and on for a few days, and gradually the girls were beginning to get scared! I played along with them and pretended I was scared too! Even the house mother was frightened. The situation was taking a more significant turn than I had imagined.

One night the house mother called the police! That night, the police sat outside across the street and watched the front door. Since I knew what was going on, I played dumb and went to bed! It was a good thing I heard that they were calling the police; otherwise, I would not have known, and the joke would have taken a turn on me!

As you can imagine, I decided to quit while I was ahead! Some of my sorority sisters might buy my book and learn of this; I never did tell anyone! They will be surprised, huh?

Chapter 5

WANT SOME PIE?

When I was a freshman in the sorority, when different events came, we were always the "guinea pigs." Friday nights at the main building on campus, they brought in bands, various entertainment, etc. One Friday night, a pie-eating contest was scheduled. Each sorority was to pick their choice to win the contest. Guess who got selected in ours? ME!

A few days before the contest, I ran into a male friend who happened to do the same thing for a fraternity the week before. I asked him for some pointers because he won that contest the week early! He gave me some advice, and I thanked him a lot.

So when Friday night came, I walked over there to the building. They had a stage set up with a long table and eight chairs, one for each contestant. When the time came, they lined us up on the scene in front of a vast audience. It brought to mind what the fellow had told me to do. When they blew the whistle, I picked up the two large pies, dumped them in a pile in front of me, squished them with both hands, and put some in my hair, some down my neck, in my ears, till it was all gone; then I hollered I was DONE!!

And guess what? I WON! I have a silver pie plate as a winning trophy. I was digging pie out of everywhere for the following hour.

Winning Trophy.

Chapter 6

THE TRAGEDY ON BEAN LAKE

One Saturday morning, the phone rang and I got a call from some friends out at their ranch about thirty miles from our house. They explained they had a terrible problem; some of their cattle fell into the lake and couldn't get them out. The river was frozen, and they didn't know what to do. I said we would be right out. Bean Lake wasn't huge, but deep in places. In the meantime, my neighbor had a huge truck, and he said he would go with us in case they needed it.

When we got there, the ranchers had called the Fish and Game Commission. They had to get approval to let them go. Well, it seems like we had a good deal. We raised Saint Bernards, and my neighbor who was driving the truck raised greyhounds for racing.

Right away, a bell rang in our minds. Why not use them for dog food? We were just looking at eight cows that figured 1800 pounds of fresh, well-frozen hamburger!

The ranchers brought a tractor to help dig out the frozen cattle. Since they were frozen in the lake, it took a while to get them out. My husband, Bill, backed up the truck, and as they pulled one out at a time, they flipped the cow into the car, putting all eight frozen cows into the vehicle. Their frozen legs pretty much just stuck out the top of the truck.

Just for fun, the rancher had an idea. For humor's sake, he got a huge banner, and we all painted a sign to put on the side of the truck. It said: "MCDONALD'S HERE WE COME!" We laughed all the way home.

When we got home, Bill backed the truck into the driveway and dumped them on the cement. We were worried about what the neighbors would think. With endless hours of hard work, the men got them all processed and life resumed back to normal, well as normal as country life can get.

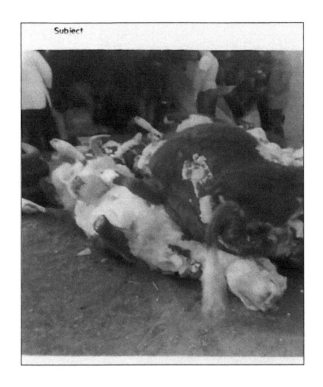

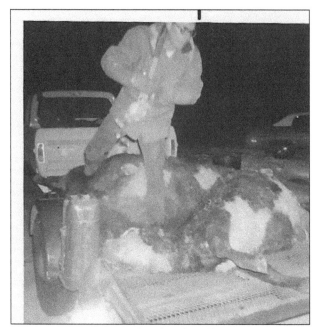

Husband, Bill Hill.

Bill Hill.

Chapter 7

CREPES GALORE

Since I was young, I always loved to bake and cook. I ended up graduating from Montana State College with a degree in home economics. My first teaching job was in Cut Bank, Montana; that was close to the Canadian border. From about January till the end of March, it was always below zero! I didn't mind it so much, as I was born and raised where it was always cold in the winter in Great Falls, Montana, but not below zero very often. I taught there for two years, then got an offer back at my home city for a home economics job for a new high school that would open that fall. I decided to take that job and ended up teaching for twenty-five years. I enjoyed my job and taught some classes in science, which was my minor in college; fun to have an opportunity to teach an additional subject.

One day, the principal came into my room and asked if I would like to go to Denver to represent the school for some meetings. I thought it might be fun. I flew there and stayed three days. One day, some of us went to lunch at a crepe place. I was fascinated with the various crepes and how they prepared them. They had crepe pans and had them on a burner, and then dipped a pan into the batter and set it on the burner; and it only took a few seconds to cook. When I got home, I kept thinking about what I had seen. The crepes fascinated me; I thought, *Why couldn't I do something like that?* I called the place when I got home and asked them about it and found out how to do what they were doing; and I would have to purchase the franchise. To buy this franchise would cost close to $75,000 to get their secrets, etc. I slept on this for several nights and said to myself, "Why can't l do it myself? I don't need them, right?"

So one day, my husband and I started looking for a building space that we could rent for "The French Concoction," the name for our new adventure. We saw a place for rent where they had sold Western clothes and boots, etc., but the basement was the only space for rent. We asked to see it right away. It was so dark down the stairs that we had to get a flashlight to see anything. There was broken glass all over the floor, and some of the walls were brick and some boards. Through all that, we got excited! We could picture how we could do things with space, and so we TOOK IT!

All of our friends said it would never work, as it was downstairs, dark, and French. There was only space for a small kitchen in the back room, but we didn't need a lot of extensive equipment. We swept up the glass, put in lighting, and fixed it up to make it into our crepe restaurant. Everything started to come together. I made server outfits with a French style. They had full skirts and blouses off their shoulders with elastic. The dresses were patterned and the blouses were white. I hired some girls from my home economics class to be waitresses, and they look spectacular in our French affair.

It was finally time to open up for business. The opening day was FABULOUS! We had people lined up all the way upstairs! Who said nobody would come downstairs? Every day for lunch, we had people lined up on the street down on the stairs. We were thrilled! Then one day, I realized only females were coming for lunch. Where were the men?? I found out they were mostly lawyers and attorneys and had their offices around there. So I decided to make some strawberry crepes with whip cream and go out and take some to these various offices. The men were delighted with what they had tasted, and I left everyone a menu. Starting the next day, we had several tables with men after that!

We understood our Montanan clientele, so we created a menu to attract men and women wanting a delicious, filling lunch. Our menu included various crepes like a Reuben, Beef Stroganoff, taco crepe, three various ones with sauces, and dessert ones. Our most popular dessert one was the flaming Crepe Suzette. We had a large gong on a cart; we wheeled out to the table and hit it with a drumstick. We dished it up at the table, and this was a BIG HIT (literally)!

Our lunch hours were only 11:00 am till 3:00 pm. So since our lunch hours were successful, we got the idea for a family night for some evening business. So we advertised for Thursday nights at 5:00 pm to bring the whole family for Spaghetti and Sauce Night. We had so much fun dreaming up new ideas and making our dreams come to reality. I can't believe we were the owners of our very own restaurant in Montana!

46 Great Falls Tribune   Thursday, June 30, 1977

CORNER CREPERY — Cornering the market on creperies is The French Concoction, scheduled by Bill and Lenora Hill to open July 5. The interior will feature French decor, and the waitresses have made their costumes in French peasant style. Waitresses pictured top

French crepery adds pizazz downtown

By LOIS MURRAY
Tribune Staff Writer

Adding pizazz to downtown Great Falls is The French Concoction, 318 Central Ave., Bill and Lenora Hill's new crepery.

The Hills, former owner-operators of the Rendez-Vous Restaurant for five years, have traveled the country over visiting crepe parlors in metropolitan areas.

"We have more than 100 cookbooks and 1,000 crepe recipes, said Bill Hill, "and I feel that we've made and tasted them all."

Flaming crepes, vegetable crepes, dessert and diet crepes — crepes with Chinese, Mexican, Italian and Russian flair and "crepewiches" are featured on their menu. They will offer 25 crepe fillings and crepes of bran, whole wheat, sourdough, yogurt, beer, potato, sweet, regular and corn flour.

Cheese will be purchased in large blocks and hand-grated fresh. Home-grown alfalfa sprouts will be used in salads.

A "Continental Picnic Board" with assortments of fruits and cheeses served on cutting boards of cherry wood, black walnut or birch, allows the diner to do his own thing at cutting up and serving himself cheeses and fruits.

The Hills have developed several cheese sauces and salad dressings and will feature a special house dressing.

Lenora Hill, author of the recently-published "The Stuffed Cookbook," has been teaching home economics for 15 years, starting at Cut Bank High School and coming to Great Falls High in 1962 and later, C. M. Russell High where she is a teacher. Bill is a winner of the Great Falls Gas Co. men's barbecuing recipe contest, and with his wife has done catering here for several years.

We hired many gals that were my High School students.
I designed and sewed all the uniforms myself.

REUBEN Popular "Business Men's Lunch" $1.95
  Corned Beef, Sauerkraut, Swiss Cheese
RATHSKELLER German Favorite 1.75
  Potato or Beer Crepe with Polish Sausages,
  Sauerkraut, Sour Cream, and Horseradish
WESTERN SOURDOUGH: The ever popular "Denver" 1.75
  Done the French way on a sourdough crepe with
  choice of mild or sharp cheese sauce.

Entreés

TRADITIONAL HAM AND ASPARAGUS ROLLUPS $2.25
  Baked ham, tender asparagus spears and cheese sauce.
FILLET OF SOLE 1.95
  Poached sole in a mouth watering shrimp sauce
ROYAL CHICKEN CREPES 2.25
  Chicken in a creamy sauce in a whole wheat crepe
  topped with mushrooms.
CHICKEN N' BROCCOLI 2.25
  Delectable, Creamy Sauce, Choice of Bran or Whole
  Wheat Crepe.   Rich . . . . but Good!
SHRIMP OR CRAB NEWBURG. 3.00
  Sherry adds elegance to this crepe.

Foreign Intrigue

12 BEEF STROGANOFF CREPES . . . A Classic Russian Dish $3.95
    A rich-tasting dish with strips of beef cooked in wine
    and sour cream sauce and fresh mushrooms.
13. MANICOTTI CREPES . . . For the Italians in the crowd . . 2.50
    A beef and cheese filling, spaghetti sauce topped with
    mozzarella cheese.
14. A Pocket Full of TACO . . . . . . OLE' 1.50
    Taco Salad with Hot Cheese Sauce in corn flour crepe.
15. CHINESE SPRING ROLLS 2.00
    A great imitation of Chinese Egg Roll
    Chinese Vegetables with a sweet and sour sauce.

16. COMBINATION PLATE (for those who can't decide) 4.00
    Choose 2 entree crepes and 1 dessert crepe

17. DIETER'S DELIGHT: House Specialty . . . Yogurt Crepe 1.25
    Batter made with yogurt and filled with yogurt
    Flavor of the day, choice of topping

*A copy of the menu we created and my talented
friend Kay Dell helped with all the illustrations.*

Chapter 8

A NEW ADVENTURE

After four years in the crepe shop and twenty-two years of teaching in Great Falls, we got an excellent offer to manage a Best Western hotel in Livingston, Montana. We took the offer.

For the first two years, we lived in an apartment inside the hotel. But we quickly found that being on-site meant they could call on us for help 24/7. We bought a house right behind the hotel, which allowed us to have our own space; yet we could still get over there fast if they needed us.

The hotel had an indoor, heated swimming pool, a full restaurant and bar, three large banquet rooms, and three levels of hotel rooms. And, of course, a heated garage for those cold Montana winters, which was a treat for visitors that time of year.

The hotel's location was beautiful, as it was only forty miles from Yellowstone National Park, which brought a lot of traffic coming and going to visit the park. In the summer, we had reservations from people worldwide to fly fish in the Yellowstone River, which flowed directly through our beautiful town. One group of doctors from Las Vegas loved to fly there in their plane. They would fish all day and bring their daily catch to our chef to prepare the fish for their dinners. Majestic mountains surrounded us, so in the winter, we had rooms full of skiers!

We often hosted many bus tours with Chinese visitors coming to see Yellowstone Park. These big tour busses would arrive in the afternoon, and our two boys helped unload the suitcases and take them to their rooms, and load them up again at departure. We served them two meals with us: the evening dinner and breakfast the following day.

One time, the tour guide reserved one of our banquet rooms for dinner. He asked if we had some kind of a dessert to serve that night. It so happened that particular day was the 4th of July and my birthday. The staff had gotten me a giant cake, so I told the tour guide I would be glad to share the cake with them. So I went back into the kitchen, and the staff and I cut the cake into forty pieces and put them on saucers. I wheeled the cart into the room, and the whole gang stood up and sang Happy Birthday to me in Chinese. I was so startled and happy that I had tears rolling down my face. I cherish this birthday memory!

I enjoyed getting to be around these beautiful Chinese people. I was amazed at how the Chinese kids and our kids could play together, even though they could not speak English. I watched them in the swimming pool, and they had so much fun splashing at each other and throwing the ball at each other, as if they were both speaking the same language!

I got to know one of the tour guides, so I asked him if he would bring me back a silver spoon as a souvenir from his travels. I loved to collect souvenir spoons as reminders of people and places I have encountered. He said he would bring me one the next time they came through. So the next time he arrived, he handed me a tiny package. It was a spoon! I was so delighted and opened it up. To my surprise it was not from China like I had imagined; it was from Disneyland! I still proudly display it among my 400 cherished spoon collection as a reminder of him.

Chapter 9

THE ROUND-UP TRADITION

Livingston had a parade down the main street and a rodeo every year around the 4th of July. It was a town effort to create an experience for an unexpecting traveler passing along the interstate and surprising them with a taste of Montana.

Some of the town's men would dress up as Native Americans with tribal makeup and costumes, including feather wood sticks in their hands. They were on horses with braided tails and war paint. They went ALL out.

A state trooper was involved and part of this whole setup. The trooper's job was to pull over an unsuspecting "family" vehicle. As the trooper approached the driver, he/she proceeded to ask the family if they would like to stay overnight with a free room, food for two days, and enjoy watching our town rodeo. Some people said yes. The willing families that accepted would follow the state trooper into town. The unexpecting travelers were led among a massive group of waving townspeople, welcoming them to this experience.

When the car stopped among the crowd, the men on horses would run around the vehicle, creating a very animated Native American experience. When the tribal display was over, my husband and I would greet the family and tell them all about the hotel, meals, and tickets to the rodeo. The families that participated had no idea they would ever experience anything like this and were always very thankful for the hospitality. Some of the families used to keep in touch for years afterward.

Chapter 10

OTO RANCH

I have a remarkable story about the OTO Ranch along the northern edge of Yellowstone Park near Gardner, Montana. A wonderful couple who owned the OTO Ranch would come to Livingston and eat at our restaurant in the hotel. Their names were Bess and Clyde Erskine, and they were in their sixties and loved ranch life. Their ranch would attract European royalty and Eastern industrialists in the summers and fall to ride horses, fly fish, and hunt big game.

This ranch was the first dude ranch in Montana. They had many friends who came and stayed a week, or even a month, to hunt and fish. At first, they had to put up tents to accommodate if they brought kids. They decided if they were going to do all that work, they would start charging. They began to build cabins, and so the dude ranch business started. Dudes returned year after year to spend summers there.

When things slowed down at the ranch, Clyde worked at Old Faithful Inn in the summer.

During their years there, they took people on pack trips on horses. Clyde bought seventy horses for these trips and hired guides. They had to train both the horses and guides. And they had mules that carried cookstoves and food.

Bess loved to play the piano from when she was young back east. She connected with a company in New York and ordered a piano, and they had to send it on a wagon with a team of six horses. Once they had to cross a river and worried about getting the piano wet, but they made it. After that, Bess would sit by the outdoor fireplace and play the piano, and everyone would sing along. The word got around, and they were so busy, they had to turn people down.

Gradually Bess and Clyde got older, and it was hard to handle all the horses, tourists, etc. They hired a family to live there and take care of the ranch. They moved into Livingston and rented an apartment. Bess was in her eighties, and Clyde was near ninety years old. One day, Bess and Clyde came into the restaurant at our hotel. We visited with them, and they inquired about staying there in the winters. Bess said she could work in the restaurant as a cashier. So in August of that year, we gave them the second-floor suite, usually reserved for a large family or a wedding.

Clyde wrote a book, since he didn't have anything to do; it is titled <u>Music, Saddles, and Flapjacks</u>. He wrote about the ranch and the trips the guides used to take. So Bess would not be bored, I let her come down to the restaurant every morning and be the cashier. She was thrilled. A lot of her friends that lived in Livingston came to see her.

Chapter 11

LIVINGSTON LIFE

WHY I LOVE MONTANA

When it's springtime in Montana,
And the gentle breezes blow
About 70 miles an hour
And it's 52 below.
You can tell you're in Montana.
'Cause, the snow's up to your butt,
And you take a breath of springtime air
And your nose holes both freeze shut.
The weather here is wonderful,
So I guess I'll hang around.
I could never leave Montana,
My feet are frozen to the ground!

(Author Unknown)

I just love this poem, as it is such a great depiction of life in Montana. When I say "winter," boy, I mean it. Sometimes the pass between Livingston and Bozeman was closed, and snow-plows worked almost twenty-four hours a day for people to get through. Since few people were traveling this time of year, we had to get creative to bring business to the hotel, restaurant, and bar.

Bill built a wooden dance floor at one end of the pool, and on Saturday nights and we had Western bands come in from different towns to play. People would flock in to dance and drink, and the rooms would fill up, and all had good times. Bill also came up with the idea to engineer a planks system that covered the pool, which created a huge room that could host significant events like weddings.

We also got the idea of having business meetings in our banquet rooms. We joined the Montana Innkeepers Association. People came for meetings from Billings, Kalispell, Butte, Missoula, and Great Falls. They filled up the motel rooms and helped other town businesses. There were 400 hotel rooms in town.

One of our favorite additions to the hotel, after we arrived, was to invite a local artist, Clarence Morrison, to set up an art gallery right inside the hotel entrance. The artist was always busy selling his wonderfully unique paintings and bronzes that captured Montana's people and wildlife's purest images. Over the years, we joyfully purchased several paintings and bronzes for ourselves, which I still get to gaze upon in my living room to this very day. My children were also blessed with a piece that they can cherish and pass down to remember their time growing up in Montana. I still keep in touch with Clarence Morrison and his wife, who now live in a small town named Clyde Park, Montana.

Beyond life at the hotel, my husband, Bill, and I enjoyed so many things in this beautiful town of Livingston. We joined some groups to meet new people. Bill was on the men's golf team, and I was on the women's team. Both of us were on the bowling teams in the winter. Bill was soon voted on the city council. Several hotel owners from Helena, Montana, which was about a two-hour drive to Livingston, came for the monthly meetings.

Lenora Hill elected to innkeepers board

Yellowstone Motor Inn Assistant Manager Lenora Hill has been elected to the 20-member board of directors of the Montana Innkeepers Association.

Mrs. Hill and her husband Bill are part owners of the Livingston motel, and have been in the motel-restaurant business for 23 years, she said.

She was elected at the MIA's recent convention in Missoula to a two-year term.

She said she plans to work for more membership and morr promotions among the state's smaller motels.

"There are a lot more places than Billings, Kalispell, Butte, Missoula and Great Falls where we could be having conventions. Livingston is a prime example of a town with 400 motel rooms which could support a good-sized convention," she said.

As a member of the board she said she will also work against proposed "bed taxes" on motel and hotel accomodations, which she said would hurt the tourist trade.

Mrs. Hill's first board meeting will mean very little time off the job and no travel, since it will be held in Livingston, at the Yellowstone Motor Inn Nov. 20.

LENORA HILL

One particular time during a meeting recess, a gentleman from Helena gave a presentation about an upcoming trip to Russia and asked if anyone wanted to go. He advised anyone interested to go to the back of the room and sign the sheet of paper. I am not sure if there was even a pause that I stood right up, almost ran, and signed the document. I signed Bill and me up without even asking Bill if he wanted to go. I guess I knew him well enough that he would be up for the adventure, after he got over the shock, and he was! We went on that fabulous trip that summer to Russia and saw some fantastic architecture, including ST. Basils, we explored Moscow, took a trail to St. Petersburg, and visited the Hermitage Museum, which had an extensive art collection. We also attended a breathtaking ballet performance.

After five incredible years in Livingston, changes were happening with the hotel investors, so we knew it was time for the next adventure. We moved to Las Vegas!!

Chapter 12

THE LIFE OF
SIEGFRIED AND ROY

We had just moved to Las Vegas, and I was planning on teaching home economics for a high school, as I had done for many years in Montana. I found out quickly that they did not offer any home economics classes. So I needed to find a job, and that's when I saw an ad in the paper that said, "Mild work, prepare meals, good job."

The next day I called on the phone and talked to a lady about the ad, and she asked me if I was allergic to cats. I soon found out that the cats she was talking about were the big, white tiger show cats of the famous performers, Seigfried and Roy. She told me to come over and interview. Luckily, it just happened I lived two miles from their estate. So I went over there and sat down at her desk with her.

In the meantime, Siegfried came in and sat at his desk, and I had no idea who he was. She explained the job, with tasks like preparing the morning meal and doing light housework. She explained that they would be leaving at 3:00 pm each day to go to their job. I had no idea what that meant, but I thought it would work out pretty well and was near my house, so I accepted the position.

She told me to come back at 9:00 every morning and wear black slacks and a white top, as they wear in restaurants. I worked five days a week preparing their breakfast; they had the same every day. They ate small meals to keep their weight down for their outfits they had to wear at night at the show. I had to count out twelve vitamin pills for both Siegfried and Roy, and set them by their places. While eating, I had to put some clean clothes in their car and take out the used ones. I did loads of washing, and I had to dust around the house.

Every once in a while, they would bring one tiger inside because of a sore foot or not feeling good or something. I loved watching Siegfried take care of them. One time the two of them brought in four baby tigers and set them down by my feet. The tigers crawled around my leg and pulled on my slacks, and I got the biggest laugh out of it.

They also had two pools outside: one was for the animals and one for them and guests. They used the pool a lot for the tigers, and, once in a while, the men went swimming also. They had to watch the clock as at 2:00 pm, a colossal truck came to pick up the tigers. Siegfried and Roy had to go with them. They took them to the hotel and got ready for the show, which started at 7:00 pm.

When I came at 9:00 am, everyone was still asleep except Roy's brother, who worked in the yard and kept it up. He would tell everyone to be quiet until the men woke up; that included the animals. They had a huge backyard and caretakers to keep it up. They had eight tigers, a white horse trained to perform, a couple of dogs, and one tiger that had been retired, but they took him with them also, as they said he would be distraught if they left him home.

I went into the kitchen and started to get things ready. When the alarm went off, I heard all the tigers making noises and stretching. I had fun looking out the window at them in their cages. Then Roy's brother came in and handed me some flowers to take up to Roy's room. Roy was awake by then and let me in. There was a guard dog in his room. My job was to empty yesterday's flowers and put the ones I brought in the vases. Then I had to go outside and give the dog to Roy's brother.

After they left, one of my jobs was to make sure everything was picked up and clean in the house. Roy's mother had a small house outside a few yards away, and Roy had told me to check on her once in a while. So I walked over to her place, and she had me come in. She was lonesome being alone, so I stayed quite a bit every time. His sister had lots of birds in cages and had me help her clean them out once in a while and put new paper on the bottom. She was a lovely lady.

The time I got to work for Siegfried and Roy was a highlight to my many beautiful jobs. I enjoyed waiting on them and visiting with them. Even after I left, I would see them here and there, and they would remember me, which always made me feel extraordinary.

It was only a few months after Roy passed when we heard that Siegfried passed away from pancreatic cancer in 2021 at eighty-one. The two men passed away eight months apart. I admit I had some tears! It is a sad time here in Las Vegas, with these two wonderful men gone. It was a privilege to have had the opportunity to work for them and have a small glimpse into their glorious lives.

Part 2

JOBS, FAMILY, AND ACCOMPLISHMENTS

Chapter 13

JOBS IN MY LIFETIME

No matter where you are or what you do, "YOU" can do whatever you put your mind to. Here is a list of jobs I have had in my lifetime: teacher, chef, waitress, business owner, author, mother, and grandmother.

After graduating from high school at seventeen years old, I picked the college I wanted to attend. I had to leave home and lived hundreds of miles away from it. The college was Montana State University in Bozeman, Montana; I was there for four years. At first, I lived in the dorm, and then after your first year, you can be selected to a sorority. I joined AOPi and planned my first job after college.

In the early days, many places posted job openings on cork boards in the hallways of schools. You could sign up for an interview. I had made up my mind to be a teacher. There was an opening in Cut Bank, Montana, for a home economics teacher, so I applied and got the job! It was minus 10-40 degrees in the winter. Oh well, it was a good job, and I saved lots of my checks.

I liked the job, but I got an offer for the next year to go back home to Great Falls, Montana and teach home economics in Great Falls High School. After four years, they had built a brand-new school, so they offered me the job to move over to that one. I accepted that job and had a class of all boys. They were so fun to watch, cook, and sew.

Jaycees Honor Community Leaders

The outstanding young educator award was presented to Mrs. Hill by Charles Clifton. She was 1966 chairman of the Great Falls Symphony Ball, is social chairman of the Great Falls Teachers Association and sponsor of the Russellettes. The award was made on the basis of teaching skill, contribution to progress and her contribution to the community.

MRS. LENORA A. HILL

During these years, I gave birth to a baby boy, Matt. And another son came after him, and we named him Scott! And a few years later, I had a baby girl named Krystal. So now my job was a mother! I will tell you more about each of my children later on.

One of my favorite jobs was as a waitress on the Las Vegas Strip! I applied for the waitress job at the Riveria and was hired on the spot. I had to take the shift that new people take, and it was starting the job at 11:00 pm until 7:00 in the morning also known as the graveyard shift. It was hard at first, but I got used to it though. It was fascinating as the people that worked in the shows and famous movie stars, etc., all came down after the shows for a snack or meal. It sometimes was even 3:00 am! It was kind of fun, though, to meet and talk to famous performers. Even bus tours went through in the middle of the night, and twenty to forty people would come in and order big meals. As time went on, months later, I got to move up to the evening schedule. I had to go to work from 3:00 pm until 11:00 pm. I made more tips because we had dinner customers and tours. Some nights, I made $200 in cash tips!

I had the wonderful experience of being a chef for the Blacksburg Marriot in Blacksburg, Virginia.

I worked with wonderful people and was able to ask a dear friend to write something about our time together on this job. Here is the wonderful write-up from Laurie Bond, whom I worked with when she was a sales and catering manager from 1988-1995.

I had the pleasure of working with Lennie when she was a chef in the kitchen. Her role in preparing food there was vital to my job. I would promise our clients the world, I would get a signature on the dotted line, and Lennie and her team would deliver, exceeding expectations every time. Lennie had such high standards, each one of her culinary works was a direct reflection of her. Lennie and I became friends quickly. At that time, I was a young woman and impressionable, and I remember watching her gently place slices of cold cuts on a piece of bread when making a sandwich. The cold cuts were folded in a sort of a figure-eight shape with frilly lettuce spilling out when the second slice of bread was placed on top. This is what made the sandwich look thicker and much more appealing, just another "Trick of the Trade" that I still do today. At this time, I had little travel under my belt and few experiences with people from other places. I found Lennie's accent quite interesting. She pronounced her vowels very deliberately, and elongated such as "Oooh WoW," "Geeez Kiddoo," "Yeeaah," and "You Betcha"! It is hard to explain in words, but if you know Lennie, you will exactly know what I am talking about. It is 2021, and through the years and miles, we have stayed in touch, and I am a richer person because of it!!!! Laurie

Chapter 14

I WROTE A COOKBOOK

I was teaching high school home economics, and I tried to make the classes enjoyable. A lot of the students had never cooked anything before. I had lessons with beginners and one class specifically for seniors I called *Foreign Foods*. This class went over really well, as I helped students pick out recipes they were interested in trying. This class sparked an interest in me about exploring recipes. From that point, I collected cookbooks for years, and, also, people gave them to me as gifts when I had birthdays.

I decided to write my cookbook and figured I had to make the recipes simple if I was going to sell them to my students. I got more interested in looking up recipes at home from several of my cookbooks. I decided to have the students test some of the simple recipes right in our classes. I took lots of notes and tried them out at home. I asked one of my dearest and exceptionally talented friend, Kay Dell Nelson-Parratt, to illustrate the pages. Oh what a wonderful job she did to bring the book special charisma and bring it to life. After I compiled all my recipes, and Kay Dell sketched all the pages, I sent them in to be printed in my very own cookbook.

the Stuffed Cookbook

by lenora ann hill

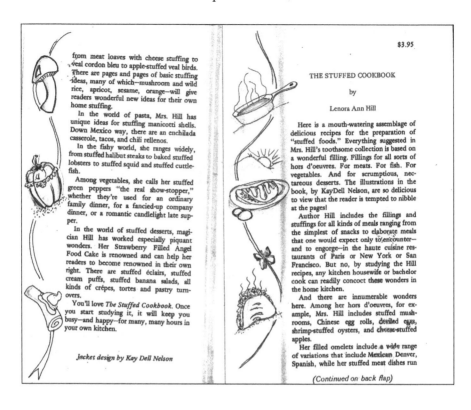

from meat loaves with cheese stuffing to veal cordon bleu to apple-stuffed veal birds. There are pages and pages of basic stuffing ideas, many of which—mushroom and wild rice, apricot, sesame, orange—will give readers wonderful new ideas for their own home stuffing.

In the world of pasta, Mrs. Hill has unique ideas for stuffing manicotti shells. Down Mexico way, there are an enchilada casserole, tacos, and chili rellenos.

In the fishy world, she ranges widely, from stuffed halibut steaks to baked stuffed lobsters to stuffed squid and stuffed cuttlefish.

Among vegetables, she calls her stuffed green peppers "the real show-stopper," whether they're used for an ordinary family dinner, for a fancied-up company dinner, or a romantic candlelight late supper.

In the world of stuffed desserts, magician Hill has worked especially piquant wonders. Her Strawberry Filled Angel Food Cake is renowned and can help her readers to become renowned in their own right. There are stuffed éclairs, stuffed cream puffs, stuffed banana salads, all kinds of crêpes, tortes and pastry turnovers.

You'll love *The Stuffed Cookbook.* Once you start studying it, it will keep you busy—and happy—for many, many hours in your own kitchen.

Jacket design by Kay Dell Nelson

$3.95

THE STUFFED COOKBOOK

by

Lenora Ann Hill

Here is a mouth-watering assemblage of delicious recipes for the preparation of "stuffed foods." Everything suggested in Mrs. Hill's toothsome collection is based on a wonderful filling. Fillings for all sorts of hors d'oeuvres. For meats. For fish. For vegetables. And for scrumptious, nectareous desserts. The illustrations in the book, by KayDell Nelson, are so delicious to view that the reader is tempted to nibble at the pages!

Author Hill includes the fillings and stuffings for all kinds of meals ranging from the simplest of snacks to elaborate meals that one would expect only to encounter—and to engorge—in the haute cuisine restaurants of Paris or New York or San Francisco. But no, by studying the Hill recipes, any kitchen housewife or bachelor cook can readily concoct these wonders in the home kitchen.

And there are innumerable wonders here. Among her hors d'oeuvres, for example, Mrs. Hill includes stuffed mushrooms, Chinese egg rolls, deviled eggs, shrimp-stuffed oysters, and cheese-stuffed apples.

Her filled omelets include a wide range of variations that include Mexican Denver, Spanish, while her stuffed meat dishes run

(Continued on back flap)

I got a box full of my cookbooks delivered, and I was so excited. Soon after the books arrived, my principal came to me and said he would like to give me a party in the cafeteria for the whole teacher staff. He told me to bring the books, and I sold them to the teachers and signed them. What a wonderful experience to see the recipes I created in print and to be able to celebrate with my friends and co-workers.

Lenora A. Hill

Teacher compiles book on stuffing recipes

"The Stuffed Cookbook," with 150 recipes for dressings, stuffings and fillings, has been written by Lenora A. Hill, C. M. Russell High School home economics teacher and noted super cook.

The book, illustrated by KayDell Nelson, a Great Falls High School home economics teacher, is due to arrive at local bookstores early this month. It has been published by Carleton Press, New York.

The text is divided into five categories, with recipes for stuffed hors d'oeuvres, meats, fish, vegetables and desserts. Hill said some of the recipes are original, some were obtained from friends and others add her touch to old favorites.

Some of the recipes are simple to make and use few ingredients. Others are more complicated gourmet dishes. But — showing her 12 years' teaching experience — the directions for all are brief and simple.

Using her recipes, one can whip up Chinese egg rolls, shrimp-stuffed oysters, cheese-stuffed apples, apple-stuffed veal birds, chili rellenos and veal cordon bleu. Seafood menus could include stuffed halibut steaks, stuffed baked lobster, stuffed squid, stuffed cuttlefish and fish rolls with pretzel dressing. Meals could end with filled eclairs and cream puffs, stuffed bananas and strawberry-filled angel food cake.

In addition to her full-time teaching job, Hill has conducted a number of adult gourmet classes and miniclasses in fondue, herb and spice cookery, flaming desserts and Chinese cooking. Her husband Bill shares her gourmet interest and the two oldest of their three children are already beyond fixing peanut butter sandwiches.

Five years ago she celebrated her birthday by roasting a whole pig in her back yard and feeding 106 persons.

Why a stuffing cookbook? She said a number of her students, former students and friends asked her for different stuffing ideas for game birds. When she found a wealth of stuffing recipes, she decided they would make a new-twist cookbook. She spent five years compiling the book, with two devoted to seeking a publisher.

The former Lenora Pfister of Great Falls is a graduate of Great Falls High School and Montana State University

In addition to her teaching and cooking vocation, she and her husband raise and train dogs, primarily St. Bernards. They live in Woodland Estates.

Chapter 15

THEY CALL ME MOM

W hat better thing than children! I was lucky in life to have three fabulous kids. It is funny how they are related but have their unique personalities!

FIRSTBORN

My oldest son is Matthew! He has always been passionate about the outdoors and loves to hunt and fly fish in Montana. When he lived in Livingston, Matt passed his tests to become a Shriner. He did a lot of charity work, like being a clown at the rodeo and parade. He has decades of experience in carpentry and has done fantastic work on fabulous log cabins to helping our neighbors with helpful projects.

He loves animals and, while growing up in Montana, we had eight Saint Bernards dogs and took them to dog shows. He and his brother would help take care of these gorgeous dogs. Here in

Vegas, he had a lovely dog and companion named Nicki; she got old and passed away. It is hard to lose a pet! Most days, you would find him driving his truck and going from different houses, being incredibly helpful to others with all kinds of needed projects. Matt lives in Las Vegas with me, and I love having him around for company and help.

MIDDLE CHILD

My second son is Scott. He has always been very driven and has accomplished great things with his career. Scott has three fabulous sons: Elliott, Ethan, and Evan. That makes me a grandma. His passion and focus are raising his sons. He enjoys taking them to Montana in the summers, and he also has a big trailer that he likes to take

the boys around for the summer months to places like Utah to camp.

Scott's other passion is restoring vintage cars and sharing his love with others. Scott has created and is in charge of a huge car

show here in Las Vegas in April. He works on the plans year-round. He has a food stand, a band with famous singers, and hundreds of car owners from all over displaying their beautiful cars.

My social life is going over to Scott's house every Sunday. I see the grandsons, and we watch football games and swim together in his pool. I cherish this time with them each week and am so thankful I have watched my grandsons grow up.

MY YOUNGEST

My youngest child is my daughter Krystal. I was excited when I heard that I was having a girl. She was born on my mother's birthday! I remember when she was born, and Bill was so excited that he took cigars over to my mom and her friends at their card party and announced her birth. It was a double celebration from then on for sure!

Krystal was always a good student and had set her mind up pretty early on to become a marine biologist. She was accepted to the University of North Carolina at Wilmington (UNCW) and set out right after high school to get her degree. After graduation, she had terrific internship experiences studying dolphin cognition research at the Dolphin Institute in Hawaii and dolphin population studies at Texas A & M University. She also worked for the U.S. Fish and

Wildlife Service in Nevada for a time after that as a Biologist. She then got married, and her path changed as she wanted to start a family.

Jim, her husband, and she have two beautiful children: my only granddaughter Emerson and grandson Colin. She has been a dedicated mother, wife, and daughter. Living in Southwest Florida, she is dedicated to her career as a children's director at a Christian church and loves people. She has been my travel buddy, and we have gone on some incredible trips abroad together.

Chapter 16

A TRUE LEGACY

It was just about one year into college when John and I met; both of us were going to Montana State University. He belonged to the Kappa Sig Fraternity, and I was across the parking lot at the AOPi sorority. His roommate, Dick Moos, had a girlfriend in my sorority, so Dick asked me if I would go with them and be John's date one evening. After that, we did a lot together as friends. Each year, school ended and we all went home for the summer. Every year when we returned, I did many fun things with John. But after graduation, we went our own ways onto careers, marriages, and families of our own. It wasn't until decades later that we reunited and we were married!

Our wedding picture.

John had two sons, Scott and Brent. We all adored John and were so impressed with his character and accomplishments over his lifetime. During his career, he got several trophies, awards, and certificates for his work. He even designed some of the parts for the space shuttles. He accomplished amazing things in his life and was an incredible man that left a legacy behind. I asked his son Scott to give his account of his dad as he was growing up. From Scott Parkins:

I think he encouraged me a lot in Cub Scouts; then was a leader in my last year, fifth grade, and Brent's first year. He then moved to Troop 56 in Boy Scouts when I moved to them in sixth grade. He was assistant scoutmaster for many years and scoutmaster for a couple. That was over seven years of my participation (1981-1987) and then for another two or three years while Brent was there. We went on all sorts of camping trips and other activities. I'd often camp with him in my first couple years, and then I moved to share tents with my friends and he camped with Brent. He bought each of us a two-man tent, sleeping bag, and hiking backpack, along with all sorts of tools, flashlights, lanterns, etc. We had a great outdoors gear collection by the time we finished, and I still have the tent and sleeping bag.

There are a lot of camping memories. They used to call the camping trips with multiple scout troops "jamborees." So we gave memorable trips nicknames; like the Freezer-ee, which was my very first one and it was cold. Really cold. The most memorable one was the "Mud-oree," a fall weekend trip to a field somewhere in Craig County. It rained all day Saturday and Sunday morning, turning the road into mud and none of the cars could get out. He and some others either had trucks or found some trucks to help tow the cars out.

He took me on canoe trips on the New River, along with camping trips, eventually leading me to get the canoeing merit badge. (I haven't been canoeing/ kayaking in years, though.) He taught me skiing on several trips with the scouts, which I still enjoy and do to this day. My best story is the first ski trip. It was at Homestead Resort in Bath County. I was probably eleven or twelve, and he signed me into the ski class lessons. And then I thought I was ready, so he took me up the chairlift all the way to the top. I guess I was scared looking down the hill, but he told me, "You are up here, and there is only one way down the mountain, so no complaining; let's get to it." He was a good skier (Montana, obviously) and had these insanely long skis that tied on to your feet. I don't think he ever bought modern ones. But he did buy me my own skis and poles. I am pretty sure I never missed a ski trip.

He also helped coach my little league teams. I played one year of tee-ball (eight-year-old), two years of slow pitch baseball (nine- to ten-year-old), and I think he helped coach at least the first two years. He also coached my little league basketball team that was my fifth grade year. I moved to play soccer in middle school, and he went to the games, but was not a coach on my teams then.

Lastly, we had a great time at Virginia Tech football games. He bought two tickets for the Virginia Tech-Clemson game that was played on October 1, 1977. My first game was on my eighth birthday. I remember it was a rainy day, but it was fun; it was my birthday. The following year, he bought two tickets for the game right around my birthday in 1978. It was a game against William and Mary that Tech won on a last-second Hail Mary. We got hooked on it that day. Beginning in 1979, he bought two season tickets, and he would go and split the games with Brent and me. In 1980, he bought three season tickets, and we all three went together to every game. I am sure we went to every home game from 1979 to about 1984, when I probably started opting out of a few games to hang with my high school friends. What is impressive is that the season tickets were front row. In the end zone, but front row. Can you imagine how expensive those tickets would be today once the team became very good? Wow. I think he dropped them in the late eighties when I was in college and could get tickets for free, and Brent was in high school. I remember taking him to the 1988 Tech-Virginia game and a couple of basketball games.

Things kind of got busy for my dad with his career. He worked at Radford Army Ammunition Plant. He was listed as an industrial engineer, which means he helped optimize some of the processes they were using to make nitroglycerin and dynamite. Due to the nature of the explosives and his contract with Hercules, Inc., I suspect he was under some level of secrecy on his job because I don't know many details about his career. He rarely talked about it at home, other than a few odds and ends. He took Brent and me to his workplace one time, and I remember he had twelve ladies in the office at desks out in front and he had his office. He could see everyone working, and all the time, he had to go out there in front and hand various workers stacks of papers to retype or do certain things for him. It was pretty neat to see him in action, but it was essentially an army/military base.

Johns wonderful sons Brent on left and Scott on Right.

Chapter 17

FRIENDS THAT LEAVE AN IMPRESSION

As I am sure many will agree, we all have friends come into our lives who help make them rich and full. My first love, Bill Hill, was a wonderful man. He had a good sense of humor, was a sharp dresser, a wonderful dance partner, and a good father to our children. We enjoyed a wonderful life filled with adventure for twenty-five years. Our marriage, like many, experienced some difficulties and, later, we went on to divorce and continue our lives apart. I can truly say that the time I spent with Bill was a part of my life that I cherish. I will always treasure my memories of the great experiences we shared.

Some of my lifelong friendships came about after going to college for four years with some of my closest friends, such as in this photo to the left end of the picture is Dick and Eileen Moos. Dick was a Kappa Sig and a roommate of my husband John. After college, I got a job teaching in Cut Bank, Montana, and low and behold, here comes the Moos. At that time of the year, it snowed all the time and was below zero all the time, so we would end up on Saturday nights playing cards at their house. After a year there, I moved to Great Falls and got an offer to teach there at Great Falls High School. But we kept in touch, and years later we connected again. Their family had grown and they had three sons. They lived in Denver where Dick had jobs being in charge of companies making dams and doing lots of hard work. Once John and I got married years later, the Moos would travel with their RV and vacation in Las Vegas, and we were able to see each other and have fun outings together.

Jeanne, in the middle of the photo next to me, ended up going to MSU also. We became friends and, years later, lived close by each other in Las Vegas. We went to the movies and lunch. We also went back to Montana for reunions. Sadly enough, Jeanne passed away two years ago and I miss her dearly. Mary, in the photo on the far right, is a dear friend of mine now going on ninety-two years old!

She is very active and is fun to go out to meals and movies together. That is me in the middle of the photo. I am so lucky to have such dear friends in my life.

Another person that has impressed me in my life has been President Waded Cruzado. President Cruzado has done remarkable things at Montana State University. She has been the president of Montana State University for a decade. I had the chance to visit with her a couple of times when I went there for reunions over the years. One time I was there, President Cruzado asked me to give a talk at our banquet with 100 people there because I had been the class secretary when I went to college there. Because of that acquaintance, we have kept in touch for many years. She is so "down to earth" when we talk on the phone about the past and what college was like when I went there. She was thrilled that I was writing a book of my life. She cares about others and keeps in touch with me often. She is a remarkable woman with a blue-and-gold heart!

MSU President, Waded Cruzado

Part 3

A COLLECTION OF MEMORIES AND ADVENTURES

Chapter 18

MY MOTHER, MABEL

My mother, Mabel Pfister, loved traveling the world. She hired a young man to carry her suitcases and accompany her on my trips. I was in high school, and I guess she thought it was too expensive, or I was too young, so I never got to go with her. But I know for a fact that she is the reason why I love to travel.

Years later, when I lived in Livingston, Montana, my husband, Bill, wanted to take our two sons on a fishing trip to Canada. They left in the motor home for a week. While they were gone, my cousin called from Seattle; her name was Lenora, and I was named after her. She wanted to know if we would like to go on a trip with her to Italy. I figured since the other part of the family took their trip, I should take one. My mother wanted to go with us, and I thought my daughter Krystal should come also. So the four of us went together. We flew into Rome and checked into our hotel. What a fabulous city, and we took several hours every day on a bus to tour around. One tour was to Naples. We could see Mount Vesuvius and many other sights.

After we had seen Naples, we decided to see some other sights, so we started with the Colosseum in Rome. The temperature was scorching that day. Our guide told us not to walk down the steps and just to stay above and take pictures. This structure was built to hold thousands of people. The spectators witnessed bloody contests and the slaughter of wild animals. Sometimes there were fierce gladiator battles. It was interesting to imagine what it was like so far back in time.

We decided as long as we were close, we would visit the leaning Tower of Pisa. It is located in the town of Pisa. It is one of the most remarkable architectural structures from medieval Europe. Krystal wanted to go up to the top of the tower; it had hundreds of steps to climb. She made it and waved to us at the top and took some pictures. When we were at home and got the pictures developed, I looked at them and couldn't figure out where we took them. I was looking down at the buildings in Pisa's city, which was a view I wouldn't have been able to see if Krystal hadn't taken some pictures from the top.

When we got back to the hotel, everyone was worn out from our long day. We sat down at our reserved table, and the menu was already planned out for our tour. There were about forty people with us on our trip. Some people didn't want to attend the tour that was planned for us; they wanted to go on their own. But everyone has to eat at the time recorded. So first they served us a glass of wine and a salad. My cousin, Lenora, and my mother were quite sleepy from the day. They drank their wine, and when the waiter brought our main dish of spaghetti, they took one look at it and put their heads down and fell asleep and almost fell off their chair! Krystal and I couldn't help but laugh, and we compared it to the Leaning Tower of Pisa! We all went to bed that night early as we were so tired.

A new day! So the plan was to take a ride on a gondola. My aunt and mom decided to stay at the hotel, as it was raining pretty hard. There are no tops on the gondolas. So Krystal and I walked down to the canal where the boats were. Gondolas are a major means of transportation; they are called "water taxis." They row with long oars. There are no streets at all in the city, so the boats are their only means of transportation. There are boats that you can row up to and buy groceries and almost anything you need. The gondolas are about thirty-five feet long, five feet wide, and weigh 1,100 lbs. It was so exciting to ride in. After the ride, we started back to the hotel; the rain had slowed down. We heard some sirens, and they got stronger as we walked. We were shocked when we got to the hotel, as it was on FIRE! The ladies had gotten out and were just standing there in the rain. I guess every trip has to have excitement!

Finally, the last stop on the trip was the city of Pompeii and we could see Mount Vesuvius. There now was a building and a museum to explain the history and the volcano that erupted in 79 AD. When the volcano erupted, it covered buildings, and most of the city was under ashes. Over the years, the covered city has been excavated and many artifacts were displayed in this museum.

We went into the museum and looked around. It was fascinating; they had a petrified dog on display, and the one that I want to tell you about stood out the most.

My mother, Krystal, and I were walking around the room and came around to a glass coffin which held a mummy of a petrified older man. All of a sudden, my mom hollered real loud, "Hello, Uncle Charlie." Krystal and I were embarrassed and pretended like we didn't know her. Everyone was laughing. She was funny. In later years, Krystal and I traveled once a year on the Viking ships and went to many foreign cities. I believe my mom's sense of adventure will be carried down to many generations.

Chapter 19

THE TALE OF THE
ANIMAL TAILS

One day my daughter Krystal called me from Alabama, where she lived. She asked if I could help her with an idea. Her daughter, Emerson, was about four years old at the time. She loved animals so much; she wanted to be one. When I asked her, "Which would she choose?" she wanted all the animals! I laughed and said, "All the animals it is. Horses, lions, tigers, and more!" Since I was a home economics teacher and taught sewing for twenty years, I thought I could help her with something.

So we thrashed through the garage and finally found the good, old Singer machine, which had not been used for approximately thirty-five years! I did not know for sure if I could even remember how to use it! I dusted it off and realized I had lost the cord years ago. So I got on the internet and looked up Singer machines and ordered a new cord. They had to check various warehouses around the country, but they found one, and we were underway with our sewing shop.

I bought a piece of fabric that looked like a horse, with white and brown colors in it. I cut it about 2 ft. and 12 inches and sewed it down the side, and then stuffed it with cotton. I sewed the opening closed and cut a piece of elastic to attach to the top of the tail, and made it like a belt so she could put it around her waist. That did the "trick"!

The funniest part was when my daughter got this brainstorm that maybe we could make tails and sell them. Surely there were other children that liked to pretend to be animals. So I went back to the fabric store and purchased four different animal prints. I also got a bag of polyester fiber for stuffing. Krystal had sent the labels she wanted me to sew on them before stitching them together. We were all set to go.

John and I proceeded to plan how to cut the tails out. I came up with the idea of using a piece of cardboard the length of the tail, which was 24 inches and the width of 4 ½ inches. This would be easier than measuring each piece with a ruler or such. We started cutting the tails but found it was hard to hold the cardboard in place, so John came up with the idea of using large paper clips. This did the trick. We went forward and ended up cutting out seventy tails from the four different fabrics.

The fabrics have a furry surface, so it is a little on the thick side. During the period of cutting out the tails, we decided maybe we could double the fabric and do two when we ended up doing, and it was much faster. The first time we did one piece of fabric, which was 36" X 60" wide, it took us three hours. After that, we condensed the time down to one hour and finally under an hour. All this was done while waiting for the cord to come; we did as much preparation as we could.

So when our mail came, low and behold, the part was here! There was much excitement in the Parkins household. Would Lennie be able to sew after not doing it for thirty-five years? Could she remember how to thread the machine? Could she remember how to thread the bobbin? Oh my gosh, what a thrill! Would the cord fit? Here goes!

Carefully, the cord was placed into the socket, and it worked! It took some tries to get the thread down the correct path, and then, OH NO, I couldn't see to get that thread through that little, TINY hole. I tried about fifty times, and finally, John handed me the magnifying glass, and, after about three tries, I got it through. So off we were to the races! Yes, I remember how to use the machine. It was so exciting. A rush of adrenaline ran through my veins, and it brought back all sorts of memories: making clothes for the women teachers, teaching "rugrats" how to sew for years, making clothes for my kids, checkered pants, and knit T-shirts (which they see themselves in pictures and say, "Mom, why did you dress us like that?")

So we started an assembly line. John's first job was turning the tails inside out. It was not the easiest chore, although it sounds like it should be. Remember, the tail is only about one inch in diameter after sewing the seam, etc. He began to think about how he was going to stuff them. Krystal said she had used chopsticks and a knitting needle. We involved my son Scott in the process over the phone, and he said he had seen something on TV once where they used a pipe and pushed the stuffing through. My engineer husband's mind started working. I figured this logical engineer would come up with something great to help us with this significant project, and he did! The following day we were off to Lowe's. He picked out a one-inch plastic pipe in the plumbing department. We had to buy the whole 7-foot pipe, but he cut it down at home to 24 inches. He also purchased a wooden dowel, which was about ¾" wide.

When we got about five tails turned right side out, John would fill his plastic pipe with stuffing, using the dowel to push it down. Then he put the plastic pipe inside the tail and used the dowel to push the filling into the tail. This process took about twenty-five minutes for each tail, but he did a beautiful job.

Now another challenge arose: We had some zebra fabric. Krystal had told us she didn't think the zebra tail was as long as the tiger or cheetah. So we had to experiment. Also, she sent us a picture of the zebra's butt to show us what its tail look like. It looked like we needed to put some kind of a fluffy fringe on the end.

We left and went to Michael's, JoAnn's Fabrics, and Hancock Fabrics to find fake black hair or something that would work. We found some suede fringe, which I bought one yard of at $3.95, but it was only about 2 inches long, and I didn't think that would work. I saw in a clearance sale bin some black yarn. It was on sale for .99 cents. So I grabbed two of those. It was kind of thin and was like an angora type. I thought just for the experiment I would get that. So off we were back home to continue. Now for the record, all we took time to do these couple of days was to eat, take a quick nap to recuperate, and get back to work!

I came home and started cutting yarn lengths of about 8 inches. I made a whole stack of them. We only had three labels left, so that was all the zebra tails we could make. That was okay, though, as we weren't sure that was what Krystal wanted. We sent them to her to see what she thought, and we might have to revise them. Later, I decided to get a thicker yarn. But would it fit in that one-inch hole? So back to putting the yarn onto the tail. Good old engineer John came through again. He dug out his masking tape. If you could picture this, he laid a handful of yarn on a small piece of tape and folded it over very carefully so it wouldn't be bulky to hold the yarn in place. I left the bottom end of the tail open. (The other tails I had to make a rounded end of stitching there, so it looked like a real animal tail.) This time, we left it open, and after turning the tail right side out, we placed the one-inch tape with the yarn inside and finished the edges and sewed. It was hard for the machine to go through that thickness, and I was worried it would break the needle. So back to the fabric store and we bought a larger needle for upholstery, heavy-duty fabrics. That worked!

Since I lived in Nevada and my daughter lived in Alabama, we had to figure out how we would do this. We had to send things back and forth. We were both fans of the Auburn college football team, and their mascot was a tiger! She decided to check into a couple of stores. One large one was at the mall, and they said if she made a good sample and brought it in, they would see what they could do.

Well, I had trouble for a while getting the tiger fabric at the sewing store, as they didn't carry much of it. I ordered a whole ream of it, and as time went on, I had to order more and more. We wanted to make it official with our "Zoo Tails" name to sell the finished product in stores and at the stadiums. We decided to pay for a trademark certificate. The trademark paperwork cost us $500. We had a lawyer help us with the papers, so we were all set. We made a deal with a big store in a mall. They made an agreement for us to get $4.00 for each tail, and they would sell them for more so they could make money.

So we divided the chores into three jobs: Me — the seamstress who did all the sewing. John — the stuffer of the tails with cotton and bookkeeper. Krystal — sold the tails, took the orders at the various stores, and delivered them.

Not only did we sell the tiger tails, but we gradually expanded to other tails also. We did the elephant tails for the Alabama games and orders for birthday parties and school activities. I got to know the postman in charge of our local post office close to our house and told him how many tails we would have to send at a time. Luckily, he had just the boxes. The height of the tails was almost 3 feet tall. If I did it correctly, I could get approximately fifty-sixty tails in a box. He charged a reasonable fee for us to send them, so we got a good deal.

The tiger tails for the football games went like hotcakes. We had fun making them, but it kept us busy, and the specific fabric became harder to find, which caused some stress to fulfill orders. It was fun, though, with no complaints.

Chapter 20

I wanted to include this story my mother had creatively written called <u>The Pearl Drink</u>. It reminds me of a trip to Hawaii my mother had taken my sister and me on after our father passed away. This was a trip of restoration and clarification as to what was next in her life. My mother was so strong, independent, and an inspiration to how I lived my own life. In her memory.

THE PEARL DRINK
by MABEL PFISTER

On a beautiful, romantic evening in Honolulu, fifteen men and women went out for the evening. After paying our guide the expenses for the nightclub tour, we were ready for our first nightspot. Everyone was dressed in their best. I was wearing a tight-fitting, pink cocktail dress that really did something to my figure. I had new pink earrings, necklace, bracelet, and dainty, pink, high-heeled slippers. The beautician in a shop near the Royal Hawaiian hotel had given me a very becoming hairdo. Wearing a beautifully white beaded sweater over my shoulder, I stepped out into the cool, soft breeze.

The large limousine brought us to a nightspot in an older section. As we were enjoying our drinks, we watched the floor show.

Geisha girls in their scant, brightly colored costumes danced, slightly elevated, on the floor that extended out into the room almost over the tables. The dancers were burlesque, making most of us feel we should have had a few drinks before we got there. Time passed so fast and our limousines were waiting as soon as the show was over, taking us to more nightclubs. After enjoying the friendly atmosphere there, we went on to another one.

At the third club, lavishness was noticeable after the first glance around. Large ferns, lush plants, and exotic flowers were arranged in artistic grandeur. Several movie actresses and actors were coming and going. The show was a variety of dances with beautiful, enchanting girls with breathtaking costumes. As we were leaving, I whispered to the guide that a few of us were going to the powder room and would hurry. We entered a room with mirrored walls and ceiling. The door to the little room we wanted to go to was difficult to find, for it was a mirror also. We got the giggles and with the several drinks we had, it took us a while to find the door. Meanwhile, our guide was impatiently pacing the floor outside. After telling him of our experience, he hurried us to our waiting cars.

Our last nightclub of the evening was just about filled to capacity. Entering, one could immediately feel the happy and romantic atmosphere. The waiter suggested a certain rum drink and said there would be a pearl in one of the drinks if all fifteen of us ordered it. The drinks were $5 apiece. That sounded like fun, so we all ordered the rum drink. As we sipped our drinks and enjoyed the floor show, one after the other thought they saw the pearl in someone's glass.

Beautiful Hawaiian girls with an orchid in their black hair were doing their native dances. They had brown, soft skin and their limber bodies were moving with the grass skirts. They were swaying with rhythm to the Hawaiian music. Their skirts were made of Ti leaves. There were palm tree decorations with bright flowers clinging to overhanging vines as in a paradise.

Our guide introduced the women to well-dressed gentlemen who danced with us. The music made dancing a real pleasure. The girls were dancing the hula and ended up with Tahitian dances. Feeling our drinks and listening to the enticing music, several of our group displayed their ability with the hula dancers. By this time, the glasses were empty and each one was looking at the bottom of his or her glass. The group was surely in a whirl, for I HAD THE PEARL!

CONCLUSION

Oh, what a life! No life if perfect or glamorous all the time. But I believe my life has been pretty spectacular because of the people I met and the experiences I had along the way. And like my mom always said: "A positive outlook makes all the difference." I wanted to write this book for so long and I am proud to be able to share my stories with you. I hope you got a little taste of life in Montana, drinking Sarsaparilla with me at the counter of a family grocery store: a sample of my prankster nature in college: glancing at the white tigers in the background while I made breakfast for my employers: and meeting some of my dear family and friends that made it so rich and meaningful along the way.

ABOUT THE AUTHOR

Lenora "Lennie" Pfister Parkins was raised in Great Falls, Montana. During her life, she had many exciting activities in the past and present. After high school, college was next for four years in Bozeman, Montana at Montana State University. She was in many clubs and lived in the AOPi Sorority house. During the four years, she received some awards and was an outstanding student and on the honor roll.

After college, Lenora taught school in Cut Bank, Montana, where it was below zero all winter. She decided the next year to go back to Great Falls to continue teaching, and she married her high school sweetheart and started a family. They had two boys and a girl.

She opened a crepe restaurant in Great Falls, and the whole family helped work there. It was a highlight in that small city. After a few years, she and her husband managed a Best Western hotel near Yellowstone Park. As the years went on, she had some fascinating jobs, and traveled the world. Then, she decided it was time to write a book!

CPSIA information can be obtained
at www.ICGtesting.com
Printed in the USA
BVHW092320021121
620554BV00020B/1032